PAST & PRESENT

CHEYENNE

OPPOSITE: This image of Curiosities, the English House Hotel and Lunchroom, and G.L. Taylor's Sale Depot of Western Novelties was taken in 1872. The building sat across the street to the north of the railroad depot. Today, the Albany Bar and Restaurant is in its location. (Courtesy of the Wyoming State Archives Collections.)

PAST & PRESENT

CHEYENNE

Jill Pope and Brady Brinton

LUNCH ROOM

ENGLISH HOUSE

G.L.TAYLOR'S SALE DEPOT
OF WESTERN NOVELTIES

1872

John Eames, owner of Hotel located
where the Albany Hotel now stands

Copyright © 2023 by Jill Pope and Brady Brinton
ISBN 978-1-4671-0996-3

Library of Congress Control Number: 2023933053

Published by Arcadia Publishing
Charleston, South Carolina

Printed in the United States of America

For all general information, please contact Arcadia Publishing:
Telephone 843-853-2070
Fax 843-853-0044
E-mail sales@arcadiapublishing.com
For customer service and orders:
Toll-Free 1-888-313-2665

Visit us on the Internet at www.arcadiapublishing.com

ON THE FRONT COVER: The red Wrangler store is a popular landmark in Cheyenne. This block burned down in 1870 in the Great Disaster Fire. It was rebuilt in 1882 and called the Phoenix Block, as shown on the building. There have been hotels and grocers in the structure. It was Baker and Johnson Grocers as shown here in the 1880s. (Past, courtesy of the Wyoming State Archives Collections; present, photograph by Brady Brinton.)

ON THE BACK COVER: The back cover photograph was taken at a parade during the 1908 Cheyenne Frontier Days celebrations. Capitol Garage, located on Seventeenth Street, is shown in all its glory. (Courtesy of the Wyoming State Archives Collections.)

CONTENTS

ACKNOWLEDGMENTS

Many thanks to Suzi Taylor at the Wyoming State Archives, where we acquired the past photographs. She is a pleasure to work with.

Appreciation to Laura Levi at the Visit Cheyenne tourism office for her assistance.

All of the historical images used in this book are from the Wyoming State Archives Collections. The present-day photographs were taken by Brady Brinton, and the text was written by Jill Pope.

INTRODUCTION

This book has been compiled from the knowledge and copious notes that I took over the 20 years that I worked for Cheyenne tourism and managed the Cheyenne Street Railway System. I enjoyed writing the historical trolley tour scripts and assisting third graders with their Cheyenne history projects. During those two decades, I took many notations while perusing old newspapers and logging what businesses were located at what location from the advertisements that were printed in the past 155 years. I read every Cheyenne history book I could get my hands on and thoroughly enjoyed many hours at the Wyoming State Archives digging through photographs, newspapers, and files. The notes on the reverse side of the photographs were informative.

Originally, Gen. Grenville Dodge, the chief engineer for the Union Pacific Railroad, platted Cheyenne in a four-mile-square grid that ran parallel with the tracks they were going to lay. The crew arrived in July 1867. The majority of development was on the north side of the tracks, initiating about eight blocks west of the depot along Crow Creek, while squatters pitched their tents south of the tracks. The first train arrived on November 13, 1867, four months after the railroad crew. Passengers were welcomed with big banners and a brass band. Cheyenne's population boomed to 4,000 people, mainly men. At the time, this was in the Dakota Territory; Wyoming was yet to be created. The railroad is the reason Cheyenne exists.

Many of the downtown street names were changed over the years. General Dodge initially named many of the streets after men who worked on the crew. For instance, Capitol Avenue was formerly Hill Street, named after L.L. Hill, but was renamed on May 3, 1887, after the Capitol Building was constructed. Ransom Street was named for Col. Thurman Ransom, commanding officer of Norwich Academy in Vermont, where Grenville Dodge had studied civil engineering. Ransom's two sons were classmates and comrade in arms with Dodge. The street was renamed Central Avenue on December 20, 1885.

There are many buildings and locations that I would have liked to feature in this book, but photographs were not to be found. Some locations have had many different and interesting businesses at the same location, and it would be fun to show all of them. In these cases, I typically went with the oldest business that I found a photograph of. The square block where the city parking garage is today was especially lively in the late 1800s. It held many shops, theaters, and saloons.

CHAPTER 1

ALONG THE TRACKS
FIFTEENTH STREET

The beautifully designed Cheyenne Depot opened in November 1887, replacing a small wooden building. This photograph was taken in 1888, and the clock had not been installed in the tower yet. Note the telegraph poles; the telegraph office was on the depot's third floor. The three horse-drawn trolleys ran from 1887 to 1892.

A few months after the railroad crew reached Cheyenne, they constructed a small wooden depot that sat closer to the tracks than today's elaborate stone building. To the east, the crew built the Union Pacific Hotel and Restaurant in 1868. The first train arrived on November 13, 1867, just four months after the railroad crew arrived in Cheyenne. Twenty years later, they dragged the wooden depot aside with a steam train while they built this lasting stone depot, which opened in November 1887.

ALONG THE TRACKS: FIFTEENTH STREET

This 1966 image shows the depot, which was designated a national landmark in 2006. It also shows that there used to be a Greyhound Bus terminal in what is now the Cheyenne Depot Plaza, complete with a splash pad and a place for events and concerts. The viaduct used to veer west and run directly in front of the depot but was redirected north in the 1980s.

The 1872 image of Curiosities on page three shows the English House Hotel and Lunchroom and G.L. Taylor's Sale Depot of Western Novelties. It became the Depot Exchange curio shop around the turn of the 20th century until 1906, when it was razed for the Becker Hotel, which was moved 44 feet south to allow space for Burlington Railroad train tracks to run through what is now an alley. Curiosities was located where the Albany Bar and Restaurant has operated since 1942.

The second Becker Hotel is pictured here in 1911. The first one was built around the corner on Capitol Avenue in 1906. The Colorado & Southern Railroad ran tracks through the alley, which required moving the hotel 44 feet south. The railroad bought the Becker Hotel at a high price, and the owner rebuilt around the corner. The original hotel was moved slowly with hydraulic jacks and became the Albany Hotel. Today, the Wyoming Business Council occupies the second hotel. (Present, courtesy of Visit Cheyenne.)

When Cheyenne was young, there were a lot of hotels with saloons along Fifteenth Street, which is across from the tracks. The Eagle Bar and the Western Hotel were built by the 1880s and remained until after the turn of the 20th century. Today, Alexis Drake Handbags is the only store on this half block.

The brick, two-story Metropolitan Hotel was built in 1892 at the corner of Fifteenth Street and Ferguson Street (later Carey Avenue) and included a saloon, restaurant, barbershop, and Turkish bath. It was classier than the other Fifteenth Street hotels. Today, this is a small parking lot.

The Asher Building, formerly the McCord Brady Building, has been brought back to life in the past decade. The upper floor houses Swiss and Pearls, a cupcakery; Asher Salon and Spa; and a party hall. The trendy Chronicles Distilling, Cash-Wa Grocery, and Cheyenne Makers and Creatives occupy the main floor. The building was constructed in 1901 for grocers and a flour dealer. It is said this was the first place fresh fruit was delivered in Cheyenne.

CHAPTER 2

THE MAIN STREET
SIXTEENTH STREET/LINCOLNWAY

In 1867, a "Hell on Wheels" tent city for railroad workers laying tracks from Omaha, Nebraska, to Sacramento, California, sprang up. This view is along the northern side of Crow Creek. Train cars carried makeshift buildings that were quickly set up, the first being saloons with gambling tables. The working girls accompanied the group.

This photograph is from 1868, half a year after the Union Pacific's crew arrived. On the left is the Theatre Comique and the large two-story Ford and Durkee Hotel, owned by ex-slave Barney Ford. On the right is the Headquarters Saloon, Merchant Tailor, Rogers & Company, Rollins House with 200 individual rooms rather than dorm style, Brunswick's Pikes Peak Express Stage, a jewelry store, and Herman & Rothschild Staple & Fancy Dry Goods. The second Legislature Territorial Assembly of Wyoming was held at the Rollins House in 1871. Since 2003, a parking garage has consumed the block.

Cheyenne's original plat was four miles square with Sixteenth Street being one block north of the tracks. Later, Sixteenth Street was known as Lincolnway when it became a section of the Lincoln Highway, which ran from coast to coast, starting in New York City and going all the way to San Francisco, nearly 3,400 miles. Lincolnway continues to be the main artery of downtown Cheyenne, connecting to Highway 30.

THE MAIN STREET: SIXTEENTH STREET/LINCOLNWAY

Addoms and Glover Drug is pictured at right in this 1890 street scene with freight teams on the West 300 block of Lincolnway (Sixteenth Street). Kent Liquor was on this corner prior to the Great Disaster Fire, which started there in 1870, burning two full blocks downtown. The brick, two-story Addoms and Glover opened in 1871. This is the oldest commercial building in use, now Our Place Antiques and Graffito's Pottery. A metal facade was removed around 2003 to reveal the original stone.

This 1892 photograph shows the new Tivoli Building as well as the Neef and Germania Saloons and the Metropolitan Hotel facing Fifteenth Street behind the Tivoli. In 1868, Theatre Comique, a popular variety hall, first stood on this corner, featuring singing, dancing, burlesque, comedy, and animal acts, followed by the Hattio Turner Bagnio. The lavish Tivoli Building still stands today, one of the few remaining Victorian structures in Cheyenne. It has a history of being a saloon, rathskeller, bordello, and the chamber of commerce.

THE MAIN STREET: SIXTEENTH STREET/LINCOLNWAY

In this 1890 photograph, the Idleman Block, on the corner, was a wholesale liquor and cigar business. Beside it was the Commerce Building and First National Bank, all still standing today. Next is the Warren Block, which burned down in 2004. At the end of the street was the luxurious Inter Ocean Hotel, which burned down in 1916 from an electrical fire. It was replaced with the Hynds Building, said to be fireproof in 1922. The Cheyenne Deadwood Stage departed from this corner.

In 1875, the opulent Inter Ocean Hotel opened at the corner of Sixteenth and Hill (later Capitol Avenue) Streets, the first to have incandescent lights. It was built by Barney Ford, a slave who escaped on the Underground Railroad. Both Pres. Ulysses Grant and Pres. Teddy Roosevelt visited the hotel. It was destroyed in 1916 by an electrical fire. Harry Hynds constructed his concrete "fireproof" Hynds Building on the same corner. Today, there are art galleries on the main floor.

8415. Sixteenth Street, Cheyenne, Wyo.

Pictured in 1890 is the West 200 block of Lincolnway, the heart of downtown Cheyenne. Cheyenne's first mall, the Warren Emporium, is at the end of the block on the right; it became the Burlington Northern Depot by 1887. Next is Phoenix Market; it has been the Wrangler Western Store since 1943. The Historic Atlas Theatre (right) remains, still with bay windows. The Cheyenne Melodrama is held here every July. The Palmer Café is also shown.

This was called the Phoenix Block after the Great Disaster Fire of 1870 because it was built up out of the ashes. The First National Bank was destroyed by another fire in 1882. Francis Warren constructed the building that was Baker & Johnson Grocers and Grain, seen here. It was the Phoenix Market in 1888, Davis and Kelly Grocers by 1902, the Normandie Hotel by 1913, and later the Edwards Hotel. It has been the landmark Wrangler Western Store since 1943.

THE MAIN STREET: SIXTEENTH STREET/LINCOLNWAY

In the late 1800s, the Abney Stables stood where the Majestic Building is today. Livery stables were parking garages for horses and carriages before automobiles were invented. Homes sat to the right of the stable prior to the Historic Plains Hotel, built in 1911 as the premier luxury hotel. The Majestic Building was constructed in 1907, originally as the First National Bank, contracted by Francis Warren. The bank closed in 1924.

The Plains Hotel opened in 1911, the first hotel in America to have telephones in every room. It was called the most prominent political watering hole around and became famous nationwide. Many celebrities and presidents stayed at the hotel. This photograph was taken in 1935. It underwent a multimillion-dollar renovation in 2002 and still operates today.

This view of Lincolnway is looking west in the 1920s. On the left is the Burlington Northern depot, originally Warren Emporium, today the Cheyenne Depot Plaza, and the Normandie Hotel, which is currently the Wrangler Western Store. At right, Hobbs, Huckfeldt, and Finkbiner Furniture Sales also offered undertaking and funeral services. It was originally known as Gleason's Mercantile and later Grier's Furniture from 1948 to 2008. Today, the Cheyenne Horse Palace is here. The Plains Hotel opened in 1911 and is still a fabulous place to stay.

THE MAIN STREET: SIXTEENTH STREET/LINCOLNWAY

CHAPTER 3

WEST–EAST DOWNTOWN STREETS
SEVENTEENTH TO TWENTIETH STREETS

Stock Growers National Bank is shown at its second location on the corner of Seventeenth Street and Capitol Avenue. It was established by the prominent members of the Wyoming Stock Growers Association. Bat Masterson worked there for a short time before becoming a lawman. This building is still underneath the facade of the Wells Fargo Bank that is there now.

Today, the West 500 block of Seventeenth Street is filled by the deluxe Lotus Townhomes, built in 2020. Cupids Adult store was demolished for the regentrification. This was a predominantly Japanese neighborhood for years. A boardinghouse, the Japanese Art Goods Store (later the Japanese Community Hall), and Carter & Crawford Café were here in 1927. The City Café and a pool hall also had Japanese proprietors. One block east was Bakers Bar, the only establishment open to all minorities.

The Davis Block was built in 1895 by I.L. Davis at Seventeenth Street and Eddy Street (later Pioneer Avenue). It housed many grocery stores over the years, including Kimrey and Nagle Grocers, shown in this c. 1907 photograph. It was later owned by Goodwill and today is a correctional facility.

The Carey Brothers Block, on the northwest side of Seventeenth Street and Ferguson Street (later Carey Avenue), housed Smith, Gutterman & Harrington; Cowhick businesses; and Hurlbut Bros. Druggists. The sidewalk slants allowed blood to drain into street from the butcher shop. This block housed many businesses over the years, including Roedell Drug and Fowlers Department Store for decades. The Knights of Pythias, a plush fraternal club, was upstairs and still is. In 2020, the structure was razed, and a Laramie County government complex was built in its spot.

An 1875 Cheyenne map titles this the Post & Cassell Building. The Leader Steam Printing House and Holts Book Store were here in 1876. After the turn of the 20th century, it became Garlett's Drug Store, then Palace Pharmacy (shown here). The Williams Hotel was upstairs. Walgreens, Karl's Shoes, Brown Shoes, and Dan Graham's Perfect Image were all here before the building was renovated in 2019 as the upscale Metropolitan Restaurant or "Met Downtown" as it is known.

The acclaimed Cheyenne Opera House, built in 1881–1882, towered over neighboring shops. Famous performers played there, traveling to Cheyenne by rail. In 1900, Teddy Roosevelt gave a campaign speech there. It burned in 1902. The Carey brothers restored the east side into commercial space and apartments. In 1961, J.C. Penney's constructed the present building, which featured the only escalator in the state of Wyoming for years. It has been RBC Dain Rauscher since the 1990s.

The Stock Growers National Bank was on the northeast corner of Seventeenth Street and Hill Street (later Capitol Avenue) in 1904. Known as the "Cattle King of the West," Alexander Swan owned a mansion at mid-block. J.C. Penney's took its spot in 1937 and was later renovated into the Shanghai Restaurant. With an addition, this area housed the infamous Mayflower Café, a Cheyenne landmark, the place to go during Frontier Days. Today, it is Bejo Asian Cuisine.

This 1930s photograph shows the Elks Club at 100 East Seventeenth Street. The club has been at this original location since 1903. Initially, there was a large plunge bath and billiard tables in the basement. Operating beside it for decades, the *Wyoming Tribune* was owned by the McCracken family for nearly 90 years. The infamous Cheyenne Club was still standing on the far corner in this photograph, and Montgomery Ward was across the street.

The iconic 1880 Cheyenne Club sat at the northwest corner of Seventeenth Street and Dodge (later Warren) Avenue. The movie *Cheyenne Social Club*, starring Jimmy Stewart, portrayed it as a bordello, but it was actually an exclusive cattle baron club. Women were not allowed. That is not to say there were not numerous parlor houses in Cheyenne. In 1927, the Cheyenne Chamber of Commerce set up offices in the vacant club. The building was razed in 1936. Today, RW Baker Wealth Management Group is on the same corner.

In 1883, Francis Warren purchased this home at Seventeenth Street and Dodge (later Warren) Avenue from Maj. Herman Glafcke, publisher of the *Cheyenne Leader*. Warren was a prominent businessman and Wyoming's first governor, serving two terms. He then became a US senator for 37 years. In 1929, the home became offices for the Warren Livestock Company, the most famous sheep-cattle ranch in the area for 80 years. It was demolished in 1959. Note the turret of the Nagle Warren Mansion at the end of the block.

Longtime mayor Lawrence Breshnahan lived in this elaborate home; today, the site is a city parking lot. It was the first house to be wired for alternating-current electricity in the United States, rather than a battery system, lighting 16-watt bulbs. Incandescent lamps were invented in 1879, and lighting systems were developed across America. In August 1882, the Swan Brush Electric Light Company was incorporated in Cheyenne. The arc lamps for streetlights were installed here in December 1882.

Prominent grocer Erasmus Nagle had this home built in 1888 at Seventeenth Street and House Avenue. In 1874, he also built the home directly to the left, which was the first all brick home in Cheyenne. The stone used was inferior, so the house has been stuccoed over since this image was taken. In 1915, Sen. Francis Warren purchased the corner home. Today, it is known as the Nagle Warren Mansion, one of the finest bed-and-breakfast establishments in the West.

Mayor, grocer, stockgrower, and banker Ithamar Whipple built this grand home at 300 East Seventeenth Street in 1883. It was one of first homes to have electric lighting and a telephone. In 1894, the respected territorial supreme court justice John Lacey, "Father of Wyoming State Bar Association," purchased it. In 1947, it became a Greek men's club and gambling hall, later reopening as a fine dining restaurant in 1996. Today, it is Hansen and Associates Counseling. A good percentage of the original structure remains.

The corner house on the southwest side of Seventeenth Street sits on the same property where the Lawn and Tennis Club once stood. The Racquet House for the club stills stands in the southeast corner of the lot. Lawn tennis originated in England and was a popular sport with the wealthy in the 1880s.

This Colonial house at 902 East Seventeenth Street was home to William and Nellie Tayloe Ross from 1908 to 1923. William Ross was Wyoming's governor; he passed away while in office. Following his death, Nellie ran for the office and won. She was sworn in as Wyoming's governor on January 5, 1925, becoming the nation's first woman governor. Nellie became the first woman director of the US Mint in 1933. The house remains a private residence. (Past, courtesy of Wyoming State Historic Preservation.)

Built in 2016, the Cheyenne Public Safety Center (police and fire) fills the 400 West Eighteenth Street block. However, Shuman Cleaners was once located here mid-block. Cheyenne Creamery was at the east end of the block in the 1930s. In 1878, the small Allen Chapel Church was built across the street; it relocated in 1881. In 1884, Elliott & Hynds Blacksmith was across the street on the northeast corner.

The old Post Office and Federal Building at 300 West Eighteenth Street filled half of the block at the turn of the 20th century. The building was vacated in 1965, then demolished the following year. The first schoolhouse in Cheyenne was on this corner. The two-room school was dedicated on January 5, 1868; by the next month, there were 114 students. A bank has now occupied this corner for many years.

Cheeks Beauty Academy, 207 West Eighteenth Street, was once the site of Ida Hamilton's House of Mirrors, the biggest, most ostentatious brothel found in Wyoming. It is shown between the Cheyenne Opera House (No. 5) and the Baptist church (No. 2). Built in 1878, it stood for over 60 years. A bowling alley was here in the 1920s. Beside it sat the Double Decker brothel. This side of the street was referred to as "the row." The prestigious Maple Terrace housing was across the street.

Yee Jim Laundry was located on the southwest corner of Eighteenth Street and Capitol Avenue in the late 1870s and into the 1880s. It appeared small with the large Cheyenne Opera House behind it to the south and Ida Hamilton's House of Mirrors beside it to the west.

This block of homes was known as Cottage Row. Gov. William Hale and Gov. Thomas Moonlight each lived in one of these; Hale's home was converted into the Gables Tearoom in the 1930s. Eventually this block became all businesses. Cheyenne Light Fuel and Power was located here by the 1950s.

The Converse House is shown here at 118 East Eighteenth Street prior to being demolished for the First United Methodist Church's expansion, which added a church hall. The home had a fireplace in every bedroom. Amasa Converse was a stockman and prominent banker in Cheyenne. Philanthropist Harry Hynds also owned this home. The Methodist church was built in 1893.

Sam Corson's "fish scale" house at 209 East Eighteenth Street was built in 1883 and is now the popular Blue Raven Brewery. The carriage house is where the brewing is done. Scottish-born Corson served two terms as a Wyoming state senator.

The neighborhood directly east of downtown is the Rainsford District, named for architect George Rainsford. His designs were known for their variety of roof shapes. He designed the majority of homes in this area and many prominent Cheyenne business buildings. He was also known for his eccentric behavior and foul mouth. This image shows his personal home at 704 East Eighteenth Street. Rainsford was very short and apparently designed the home with that in mind. His barn was attached.

This building is located at 520 West Nineteenth Street at the northeast corner of Nineteenth Street and O'Neil Avenue. Gus Fleischli, a Studebaker dealer, constructed the building in 1950. The place became Vern Hagestadt Lincoln-Mercury and then Vern Hagestadt Volkswagen. Later, it was converted into Pioneer Printing through 2017. The business itself operated in Cheyenne for over 100 years, opening in 1889. Blacktooth Brewing renovated the empty building and opened here in 2020, still featuring its original terrazzo floor.

The Dildine Garage was located at 313–323 West Nineteenth Street in the 1920s. Its advertisement stated it was a Studebaker distributor. In 1943, it became Walton Motors. The business was razed in 1970. It became the drive-through for Bank of the West.

Central School was built at Central Avenue and Twentieth Street in 1871, serving grades 1 through 12 until 1890, when Cheyenne High School opened at the southwest corner of Central Avenue and Twenty-Second Street behind the Carnegie Library. This image was taken in 1886.

CHAPTER 4

NORTH–SOUTH DOWNTOWN STREETS

THOMES, PIONEER, AND CAREY AVENUES

The Dinneen brothers operated a grocery and owned the Bon-Ton Livery stables at the southwest corner of Sixteenth Street and Eddy Street (later Pioneer Avenue) in 1890. They established Dinneen Motors in 1906, then moved across the street to the north in 1927 when the Whitehead buildings were demolished. They consistently adapted to changing transportation needs of the community through 2006.

Turner Hall or Turn Verein was a German men's fraternal society located on the corner of Lincolnway and Thomes Avenue. It was built in 1891. The hall included a bar, a club room, a stage and balcony, and a gymnasium with athletic equipment. It even had a trapeze. The hall also featured an opulent ballroom. Galas, bazaars, and various public events were held there. It was lost to fire in 1940. The Eagles built a smaller modern lodge in its place.

This photograph of the Frank G. Smith Motor Company was taken in 1924. It was located at 1712 Thomes Avenue. Today, this is the police department parking lot.

Ellsworth Kansas Cream Flour and Peabody's Grocery were located at 1917 Thomes Avenue in 1915. Today, this same block is filled by the Cheyenne Civic Center. The Read Block is on the west side of the 1900 block of Thomes Avenue.

The Whitehead Building is known as the first wooden store constructed in Cheyenne; however, the 1868 city directory stated that the first building was a saloon that went up one block east of this location at the corner of Sixteenth (later Lincolnway) and Eddy Street (later Pioneer Avenue). The Whitehead Building was condemned in 1912. The Dinneens operated their automobile sales business here until 2009. Today, the impressive Wyoming Rib and Chop House is on this corner.

The McDaniel Saloon and Gambling House opened in October 1867 at Eddy Street (later Pioneer Avenue) and Sixteenth Street. It burned down eight years later. McDaniel rebuilt in the same square block. He advertised "1001 marvels," featuring Charlotte Temple, the "English Giantess," who stood seven feet tall and weighed 400 pounds. He presented Shakespeare plays and operas. Every night, a band would perform outside, and men would gather and then mosey inside. Later, the *Daily Sun* newspaper operated in the building. Today, this is a parking garage.

Tim Dyer opened Dyer's Hotel in 1868 on the west side of Eddy Street (later Pioneer Avenue) north of the Whitehead Building where a parking lot is today. It burned down in the Great Disaster Fire in 1870. Dyer rebuilt on this block, but another fire hit five years later, so the third one was constructed of brick. Buffalo Bill and Wild Bill Hickok stayed there. It operated for 58 years. Frenchy's Saloon sat beside it to the north.

At 2020 Eddy Street (later Pioneer Avenue), a magnificent home was built by Joseph Carey. It was later purchased by surveyor, merchant, and rancher Henry Hay. For many years, this served as a private mental asylum, and it was later the Shingle apartments before being torn down. A dry cleaner and the Liquor Locker were in this location prior to the US Bank moving in.

The square block where a parking garage stands today was one of the liveliest at Cheyenne's inception. This 1880s image shows the Union Mercantile Company, owned by Erasmus Whipple and Henry Hay. It became the Princess and later the WYO Movie Theatre from the 1920s to the 1960s. The popular Capitol Saloon was also on this block. It was razed in 1973 for a city parking lot.

Prior to the T.A. Kent Bank, built in 1882, the First Territorial Assembly met in a small wooden building at the southwest corner of Eddy Street (later Pioneer Avenue) and Seventeenth Street. There it passed a resolution to grant women the right to vote and hold public office, being the first in the nation to allow women these rights in 1869. Today, the Mini Mall is on this corner, the west side of the building adorned with a suffragette mural to commemorate this historic event.

Thomas Kent's home was located at 2120 Carey Avenue. He owned the liquor store where the Great Disaster Fire started in 1870. Apparently, he recovered from the loss, as the previous page shows the bank he operated, although the bank went belly up in 1893. This home had also been owned by J.H. "Henty" Arp, owner of Arp Hardware. The Long office building went up in 2006 after demolishing Harry's Pizza and the Draper home to the south.

The northeast corner of Ferguson Street (later Carey Avenue) and Eighteenth Street held a Presbyterian church. There were churches on two more corners at this intersection in 1869. By 1902, Moses Keefe had constructed Keefe Hall, later connecting the church to his hall. It was used for galas, festivals, and lectures. It also had a skating rink and a porch where musicians could play. Prisoners from the Johnson County War were housed there during the trial. The ever-popular Club Araby was there in the 1930s but was demolished in the 1970s.

The original courthouse was built at the corner of Nineteenth Street and Ferguson Street (later Carey Avenue) as seen here in 1873. It was razed in 1917, and a replacement went up in the same location. In 1995, a new government complex was added onto the north side, filling the entire block. The original city jail was part of the courthouse. Alfred Packer, a known cannibal, and Calamity Jane were held in this jail. Tom Horn was hanged for murder on this block.

Before the government complex filled the block, there was a European-style castle at this location. It was built by cattle baron Alexander Swan as a wedding present for his daughter Louise in 1886. However, he went bankrupt, and it was purchased by shyster David Dare, who had the construction completed. It served as Schrader's Funeral Home before the funeral home moved into the Idleman Mansion. Schrader's tried to have the castled moved in 1963, but it crumbled.

George Draper's large home was built for his family along Millionaire's Row on Ferguson Street (later Carey Avenue). From 1895 to 1898, the home served as the governor's mansion for Gov. William Richards, owner of the Lazy D Ranch. N.R. Davis then bought the home. It was demolished around 2005 to make space for the Tom Long Building parking lot. The keystones from the Draper home are used in the first-floor windows of the new Long Building.

Joseph Carey came to Cheyenne as the US attorney for the Wyoming Territory. He served in Congress as a territorial representative and was elected the first US senator from Wyoming in 1890. He then served as the governor of Wyoming from 1911 to 1915. He built the most opulent home on Millionaire's Row, filling the entire block. It served as the governor's mansion during his term. Today, there is a federal building in its spot.

Ferguson Street (later Carey Avenue) was known as Millionaire's Row as it was lined with elaborate homes. Today, nearly all of the homes are gone, and they have been replaced with commercial businesses. East Seventeenth Street also had many large, elaborate homes. A modernization trend hit in the 1950s and 1960s. As the Cheyenne business district grew, a lot of homes were demolished, and several businesses were covered with modern metal facades.

Liquor distributor Max Idleman had his home built at Twenty-Fourth Street and Ferguson Street (later Carey Avenue) in 1887. It had eight fireplaces, each of stone or marble imported from a different country. The turret window attaches to the ballroom with velvet-covered bench seats along the walls. It was home to Gov. DeForest Richards from 1893 to 1903. Schraeder's Funeral Home operated here for decades. The funeral home added a modern chapel to the front. In 2015, it became a state office building.

NORTH–SOUTH DOWNTOWN STREETS

CAPITOL, CENTRAL, AND WARREN AVENUES

This Hill Street (later Capitol Avenue) image was taken from the depot building in 1890. There were many homes lining the street; today, it is all businesses. The Warren Emporium (right) was converted into the Burlington Railroad Depot in 1887. It is now the Cheyenne Depot Plaza and is used for events. The white Inter Ocean Hotel can be seen across from the Phoenix Market, today's Wrangler Western Store. Today, the Hynds Building replaces the Inter Ocean Hotel on this corner.

Francis Warren was a Wyoming senator for 37 years. He was a founding father of Cheyenne and seemed to have his hand in everything. He built nine large commercial buildings in Cheyenne, including the 1884 Warren Emporium, which was a mall with 24 stores. Burlington Northern purchased the emporium and renovated it into a train depot. In 1929, the railroad built a modern depot in the same location. It was there until 1955, when the tracks were removed.

This view is looking south on Capitol Avenue from mid-block between Sixteenth and Seventeenth Streets. The Capitol Theatre was built in 1905. In 1930, it became the Paramount Movie Theatre, regentrified today as the trendy Paramount Café and Ballroom. The Warren Emporium/Burlington Northern Depot can be seen past the theater at left with the depot in the back. The Hynds Building is across the street (right) from the theater, and the Normandie Hotel is across from the Hynds. Today, the hotel is the Wrangler Western Store.

The *Daily Leader* was Cheyenne's first newspaper, established by Warren Richardson. It had a few different locations; in 1907, it was located at 1612 Capitol Avenue, as seen in the photograph. A barbershop was located here in the 1920s, then Phoenix Books was here for many years. In 2022, Downtown Vinyl record store was housed here.

Cheyenne Light Fuel and Power has had a few locations in town. It is at 1706 Capitol Avenue in this image. In the 1950s, it was around the corner on Eighteenth Street, which was formerly known as Cottage Row.

The Rocky Mountain Telephone Building, at the southeast corner of Seventeenth Street and Capitol Avenue, was built in 1906 with two floors; the third floor, seen in this 1929 photograph, was added later. Cheyenne had telephones in 1878, less than three years after Bell invented them. Over the years, the upper floors housed a hotel, and the main level was a shoe store and an optical clinic prior to becoming Glen Garrett Architecture. Note the Cheyenne Business College behind it.

This 1920s Capitol Avenue street scene shows the Rocky Mountain Telephone Building (1623 Capitol Avenue), Stock Growers National Bank (1701 Capitol Avenue), Glendale Hotel (1717 Capitol Avenue), the Alert Fire Company, seen with a spire (1715 Capitol Avenue), and the entrance to Windsor Hotel (1721½ Capitol Avenue).

Wyoming was the first state to allow women the right to vote. Cheyenne women were the second to legally vote in the country following Laramie, Wyoming. In 1888, they voted at the Alert Fire Company. A commemorative suffragette boot designates the voting spot today. The fire company building was constructed in 1877. "We Strive to Save" was engraved over the arched window. Later, it became a Greek men's club before being demolished in the 1960s.

The second Masonic temple was built on the west side of the 1900 block of Capitol Avenue in 1901. It was a majestic building. It had a bowling alley. There was a terrible electric fire on a cold winter night in 1903 that gutted the building and roof. Fortunately, the outer walls remained intact, and the Masons were able to rebuild. The new building does not have the spires, though. An addition was built in 1911 adding a gymnasium, auditorium, and stage.

The Emerson Building, named for Gov. Frank Emerson, houses Wyoming state offices on the northeast corner of Capitol Avenue and Twentieth Street. The state purchased the building in 1975. Originally, this was Lulu McCormick Junior High, built in 1928 with 38 classrooms.

Carnegie Library, Cheyenne, Wyo.

Cheyenne's first library was created in a small third-floor room in 1886. Philanthropist Andrew Carnegie gifted Cheyenne $50,000 used to build the very first county library in the United States, which opened in 1902. It was located at 2119 Capitol Avenue. Unfortunately, it was demolished in 1971. Later, a bank was constructed in its spot. The bank has been renovated into administrative offices for St. Mary's Cathedral, which stands south of the offices.

The Richardsons and their seven children lived in an affluent Victorian mansion at 2220 Capitol Avenue. The family owned the opulent Tivoli Saloon and were involved in the newspaper and oil industry, along with many other holdings. Richardson scholarships are still given at the University of Wyoming and Casper College, and the family paid for a wing at the hospital. The current Hathaway Federal Building was constructed over a century ago in 1899 in the same location where the Richardson home once stood.

The Union Pacific Railroad gifted Cheyenne the land from Hill Street (later Capitol Avenue) to Dodge (later Warren) Avenue and Twenty-Second to Twenty-Fourth Streets for the Union Pacific Park. It was still the Wild West, and citizens had to put a fence around the area because the cattle herds kept tromping through the park. Today, the Wyoming Supreme Court Building, constructed in 1937, and the Barrett State Office Building occupy the former four-block park.

Construction of the Wyoming State Capitol began on the edge of the prairie in 1886, four years before Wyoming legally became a state. The second phase of construction was completed in 1890, which added a wing on the east and the west sides of the Capitol and coincided with statehood. In 1915, the legislature approved construction of the House and Senate chambers, which took two years to build. A five-year restoration project was completed in 2019.

The 1910 Gleason Mercantile Building, another structure constructed by Francis Warren, sits at the northeast corner of Central Avenue and Lincolnway. Later, it became Warren Mercantile and then Hobbs, Huckfeldt, and Finkbiner, who mixed furniture sales with undertaking and had a mortuary in the basement. A beautiful half-moon stained-glass window graced the main-floor chapel. R.S. Grier purchased the store in 1948 and operated it as Grier Furniture until 2008. The Cheyenne Horse Palace occupies the building today.

The Lincoln Theatre was built in 1929 at 1615 Central Avenue. An advertisement in the June 11, 1912, *Wyoming Tribune* for Mrs. Wards Store promoted "the Gossard Corsets [that] lace in front" at this same address. The Lincoln Theatre was remodeled in 1953. Today, it has been regentrified into a trendy music venue called The Lincoln.

The Deming Building, at the southwest corner of Seventeenth Street and Central Avenue, was constructed in 1911, the same year as the Plains Hotel, which stood south of this structure. The Cheyenne Business College was incorporated in the 1890s in another location. The Central Avenue location closed in the 1930s, but ghost signs for the Cheyenne Business College can still be seen on the upper west-side bricks. The Wyoming Lottery Corporation has been here since August 2014.

In 1890, Cheyenne High School opened at the southwest corner of Central Avenue and Twenty-Second Street, behind the Carnegie Library. Girls were to enter through the Central Avenue door, and boys used the rear entrance off Twenty-Second Street. It was used as a school until 1922 and eventually demolished in 1964 for a parking lot. A new high school was built at Warren Avenue and Twenty-Eighth Street.

The square block of Central Avenue to Warren Avenue and Twenty-Fourth to Twenty-Fifth Streets was purchased by St. John's Catholic Church in 1885 for a school that opened in January 1886. It later became St. Mary's School with student boarding and a convent. The name changed a couple times, and more buildings were added, but it remained a Catholic academy until it was demolished in 2010, when the State of Wyoming purchased the land.

The historic Wyoming Governor's Mansion, at the northeast corner of Twenty-First Street and House Avenue, was home to 19 governors from 1905 to 1976, when a new mansion was built north of town. In 1890, the Wyoming Legislature authorized construction of a mansion, but it did not appropriate funds for another 11 years. The modest home was built in 1904 in an existing neighborhood, among the people and without a fence. Nellie Tayloe Ross, the nation's first woman governor, lived here.

The Union Pacific donated land for St. John's Hospital, seen here at Twenty-Third Street and House Avenue, built in 1882. Cheyenne's first hospital was in a tent in front of the depot. Then there was a small second-floor hospital on Ferguson (Carey) Street where patients often had to share a bed. Upgrades, additions, and renovations have been made over the past century. It became Memorial Hospital and today is the state-of-the-art United Regional Medical Center.

DISCOVER THOUSANDS OF LOCAL HISTORY BOOKS FEATURING MILLIONS OF VINTAGE IMAGES

Arcadia Publishing, the leading local history publisher in the United States, is committed to making history accessible and meaningful through publishing books that celebrate and preserve the heritage of America's people and places.

Find more books like this at
www.arcadiapublishing.com

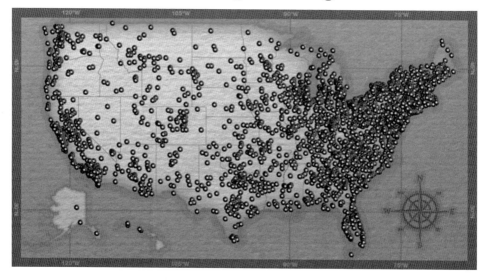

Search for your hometown history, your old stomping grounds, and even your favorite sports team.

Consistent with our mission to preserve history on a local level, this book was printed in South Carolina on American-made paper and manufactured entirely in the United States. Products carrying the accredited Forest Stewardship Council (FSC) label are printed on 100 percent FSC-certified paper.

MADE IN THE USA